THE AMAZING
GIVING TREE SECRET

A Story of Kindness, Love, & Joy

[signature: Mary E. Fimbel]

Written by MARY ELLEN FIMBEL

Illustrated by KATHY KERBER

CrossBooks™
A Division of LifeWay
1663 Liberty Drive
Bloomington, IN 47403
www.crossbooks.com
Phone: 1-866-879-0502

©2013 Mary Ellen Fimbel. All rights reserved.

No part of this book may be reproduced, stored in a retrieval system, or transmitted by any means without the written permission of the author.

First published by CrossBooks 11/19/2013

ISBN: 978-1-4627-0644-0 (sc)
ISBN: 978-1-4627-1782-8 (e)

Printed in the United States of America

This book is printed on acid-free paper.

Certain stock imagery © Thinkstock.
Any people depicted in stock imagery provided by Thinkstock are models, and such images are being used for illustrative purposes only.

Because of the dynamic nature of the Internet, any web addresses or links contained in this book may have changed since publication and may no longer be valid. The views expressed in this work are solely those of the author and do not necessarily reflect the views of the publisher, and the publisher hereby disclaims any responsibility for them.

To the honor and glory of God.
May His gifts of kindness, love,
and joy abide in your hearts.

In loving memory of our grandson, Andrew Fimbel.
May he rest peacefully in Jesus' arms.

To our precious grandchildren: Richie, Christy, Caleb, Brayden,
Luke, and Aliyah Fimbel, who are the sunshine of our lives.

Andrew's Toy Box (www.andrewstoybox.org) is a non-profit, federally approved, charitable organization which provides toys and gifts to sick children in the United States and throughout the world. This charity was founded in 2001 in loving memory of Andrew Fimbel.

Proceeds from The Amazing Giving Tree Secret will benefit Andrew's Toy Box.

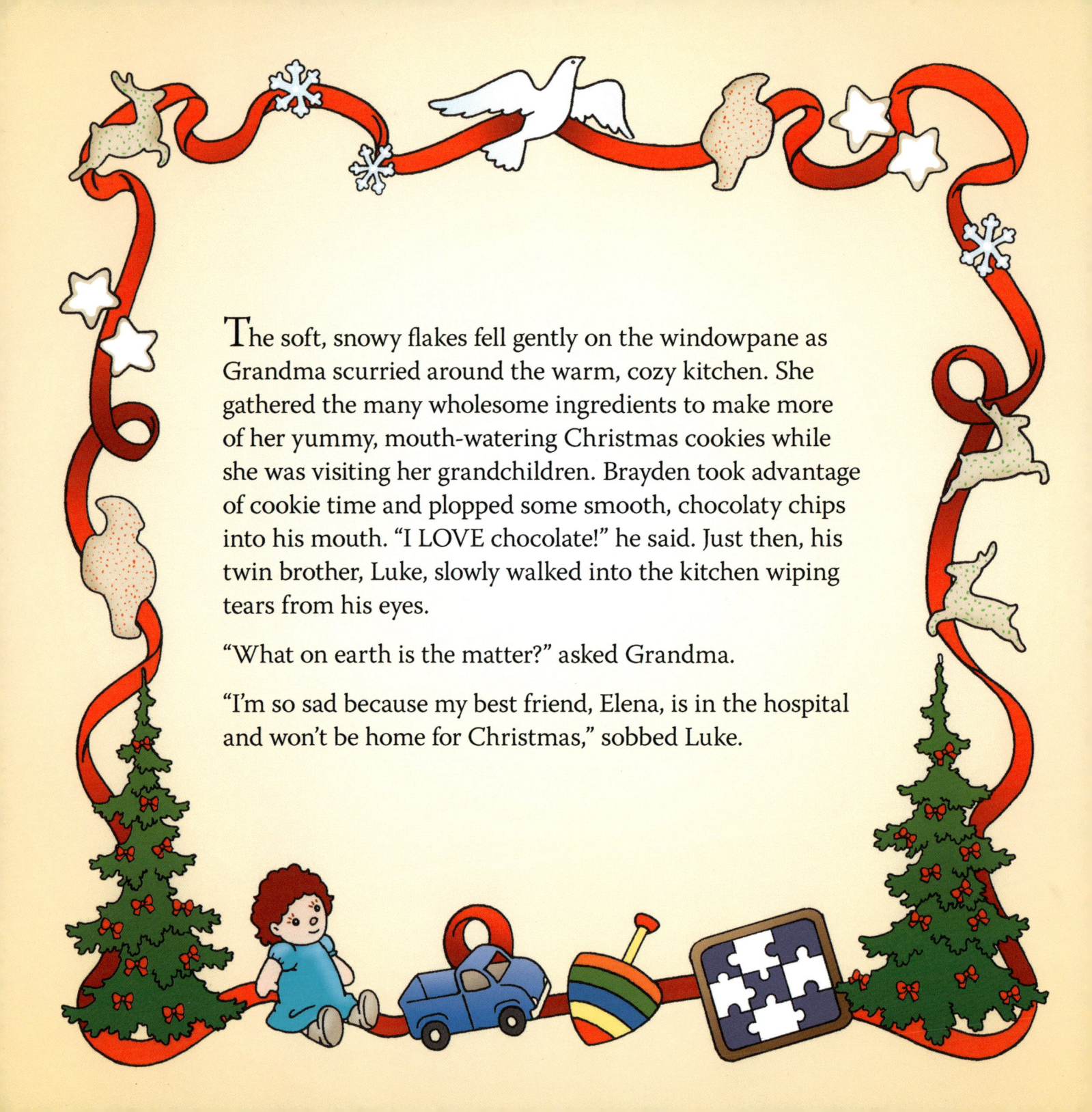

The soft, snowy flakes fell gently on the windowpane as Grandma scurried around the warm, cozy kitchen. She gathered the many wholesome ingredients to make more of her yummy, mouth-watering Christmas cookies while she was visiting her grandchildren. Brayden took advantage of cookie time and plopped some smooth, chocolaty chips into his mouth. "I LOVE chocolate!" he said. Just then, his twin brother, Luke, slowly walked into the kitchen wiping tears from his eyes.

"What on earth is the matter?" asked Grandma.

"I'm so sad because my best friend, Elena, is in the hospital and won't be home for Christmas," sobbed Luke.

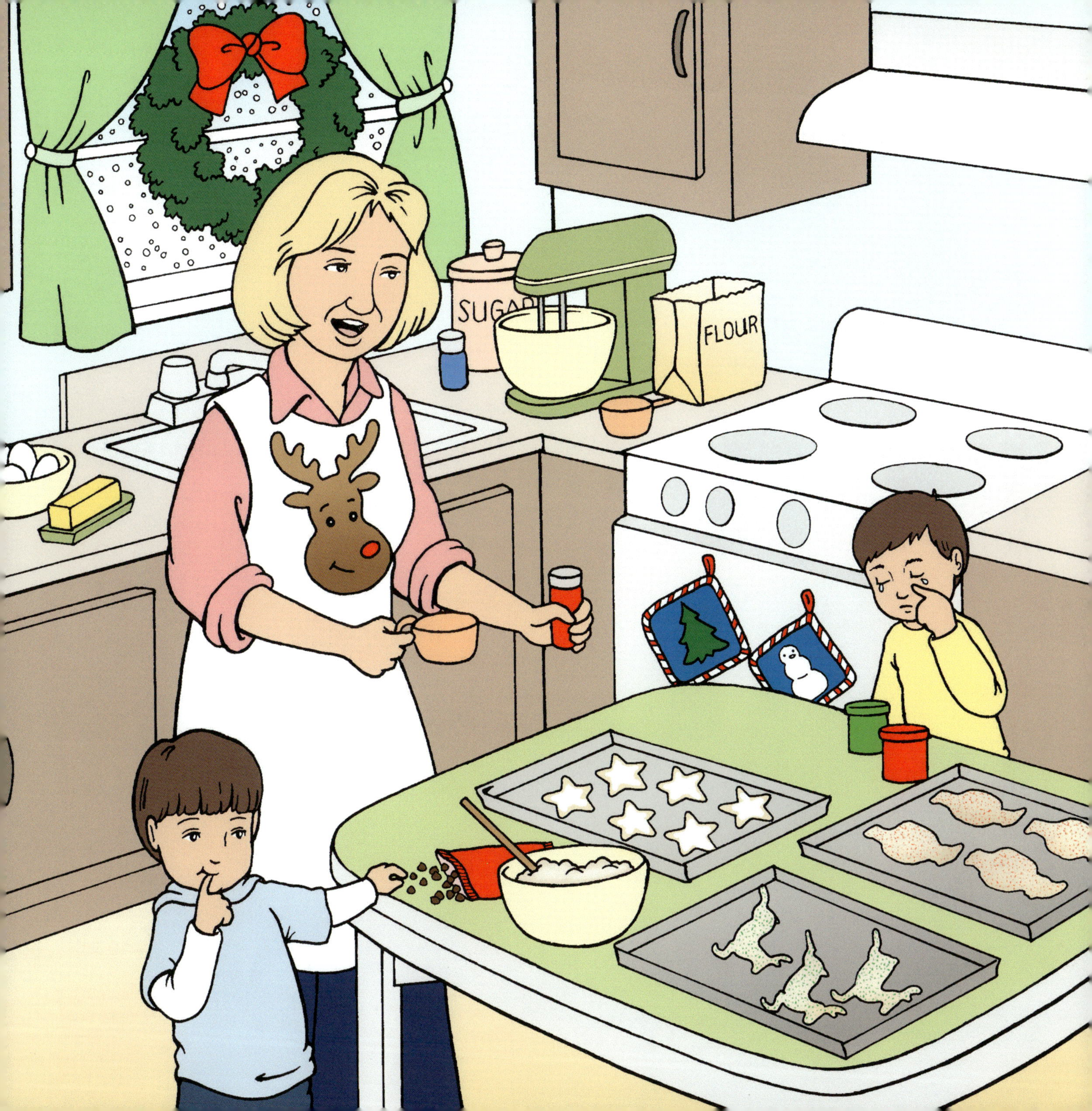
SUGAR
FLOUR

"If only we could do something to cheer her up," said Brayden. He sat silently staring outside into the winter wonderland. Then, suddenly, he jumped up and said, "I got it, let's take some cookies to Elena."

Luke perked up and said, "What a great idea!" Even baby sister Aliyah cooed happily from her high chair.

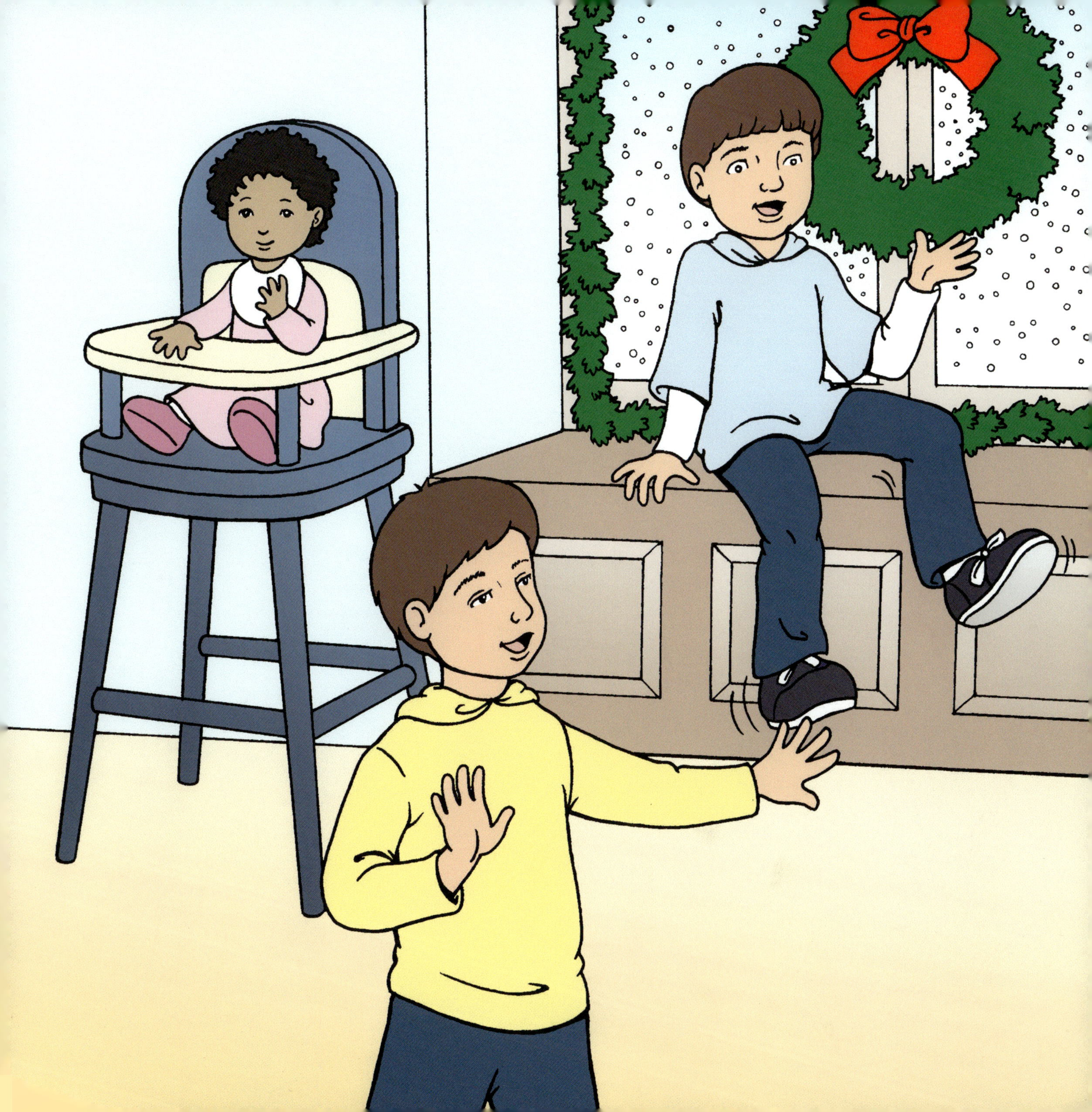

Grandma shared the boys' excitement about bringing some cookies to Elena as she pulled the last batch from the oven. "Elena will love the fancy cookies that you both decorated earlier today. Grandpa, get the car started," she said. "Boys, hurry and put on your jackets, mittens, and hats. We need to go to the hospital now."

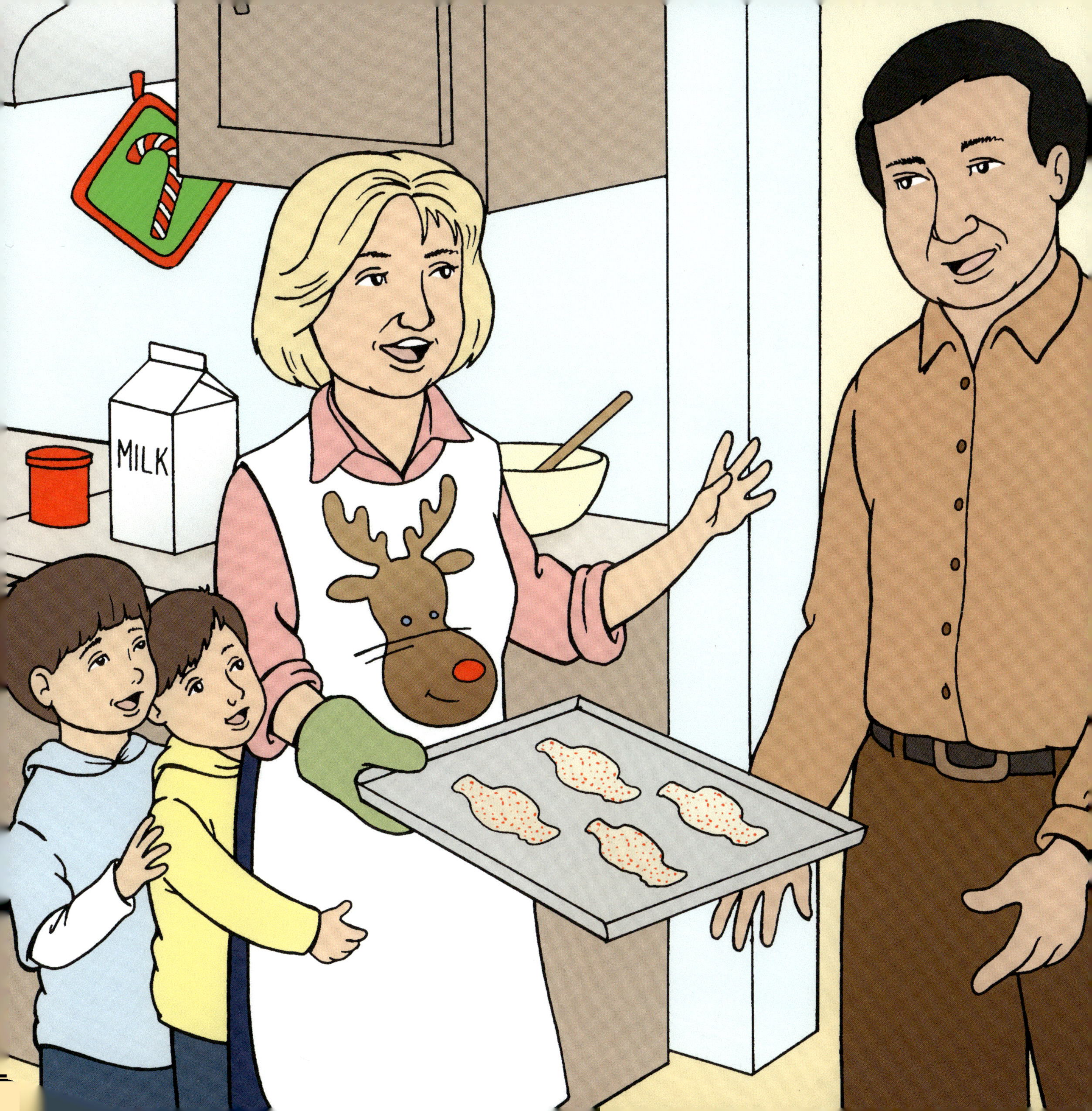
MILK

The boys entered the hospital where Elena was staying and passed many children on the way to her room. "Look," said Brayden, "there's a boy in a wheelchair and a baby girl with a cast on her arm."

"I see," replied Luke, " it must be hard to stay in a wheelchair and not be able to walk." When they came to Elena's room, the twins saw a girl hobble by on crutches.

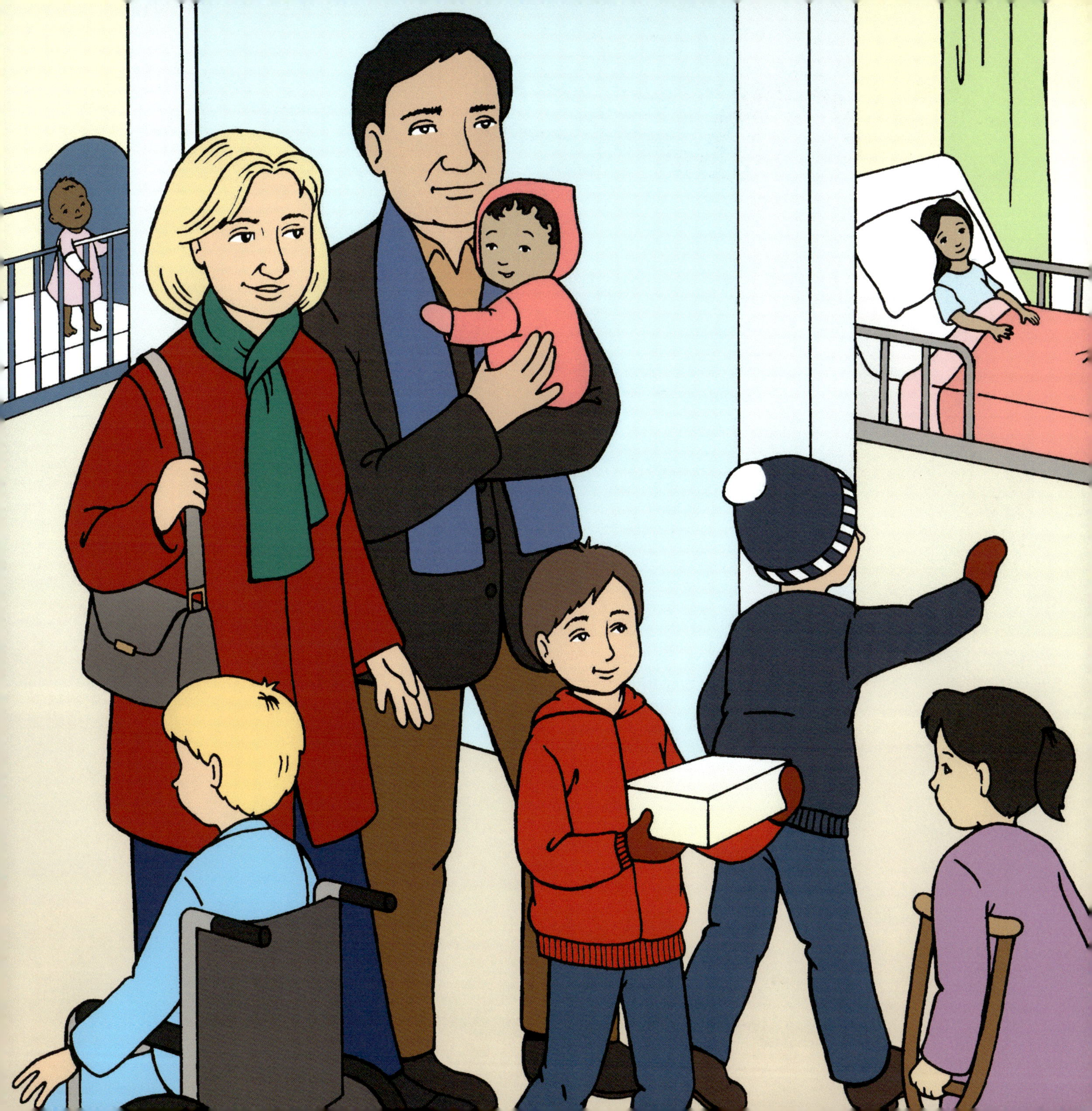

Elena looked pale and tired, but slowly a smile crept onto her shy little face. "I am so happy to see you; I miss being with you at school and playing games at recess. I wish I could go home for Christmas," she quietly said.

"We have brought you some of our super special Christmas cookies," said Brayden proudly. "My santa and reindeer have more sprinkles than Luke's."

"No way," said Luke, "my snowflakes and stars have more icing than yours, Brother!"

Elena softly giggled and said, " I love all of your yummy cookies! I will share them with my friends who will also be staying in the hospital until they are better."

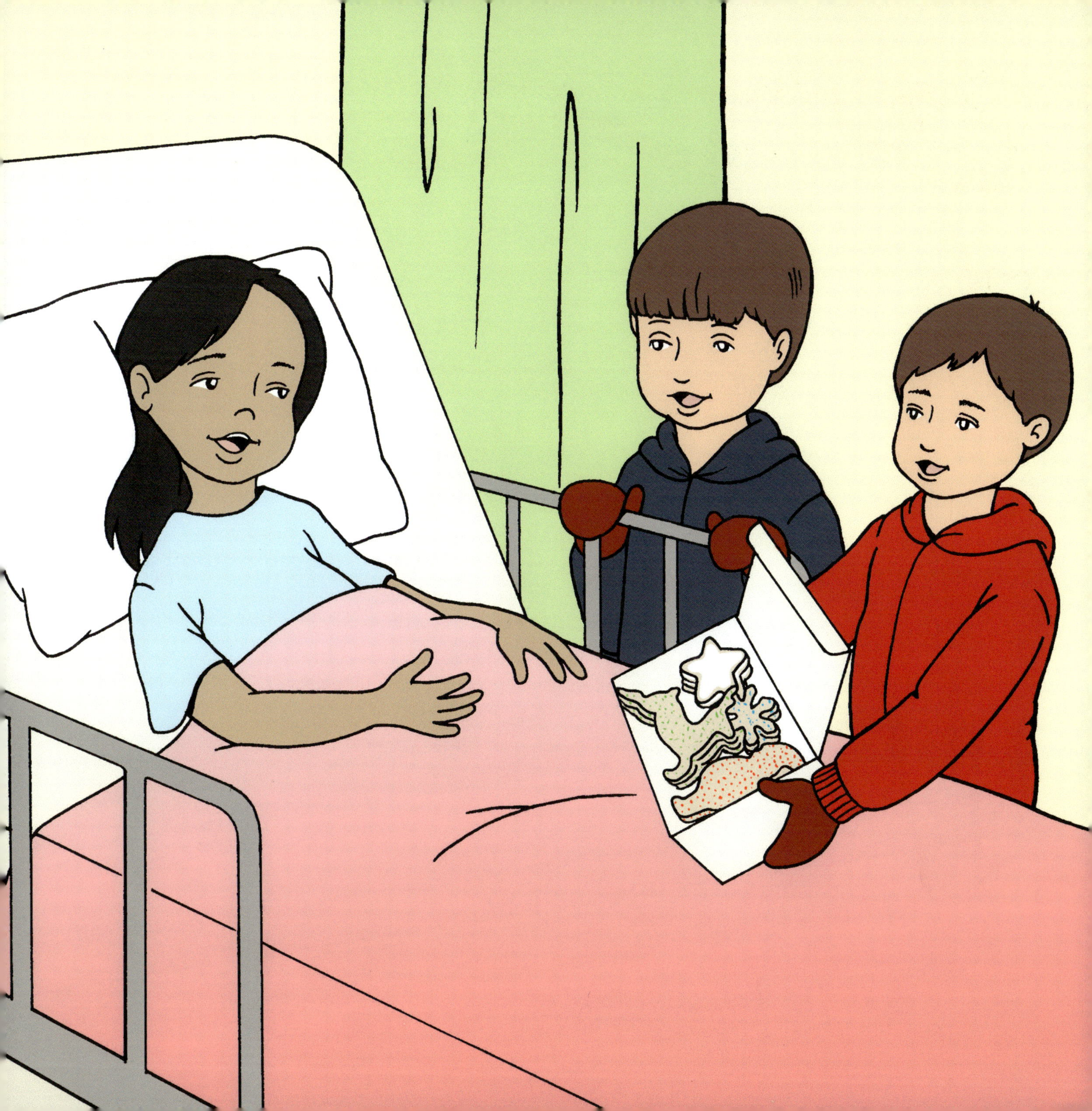

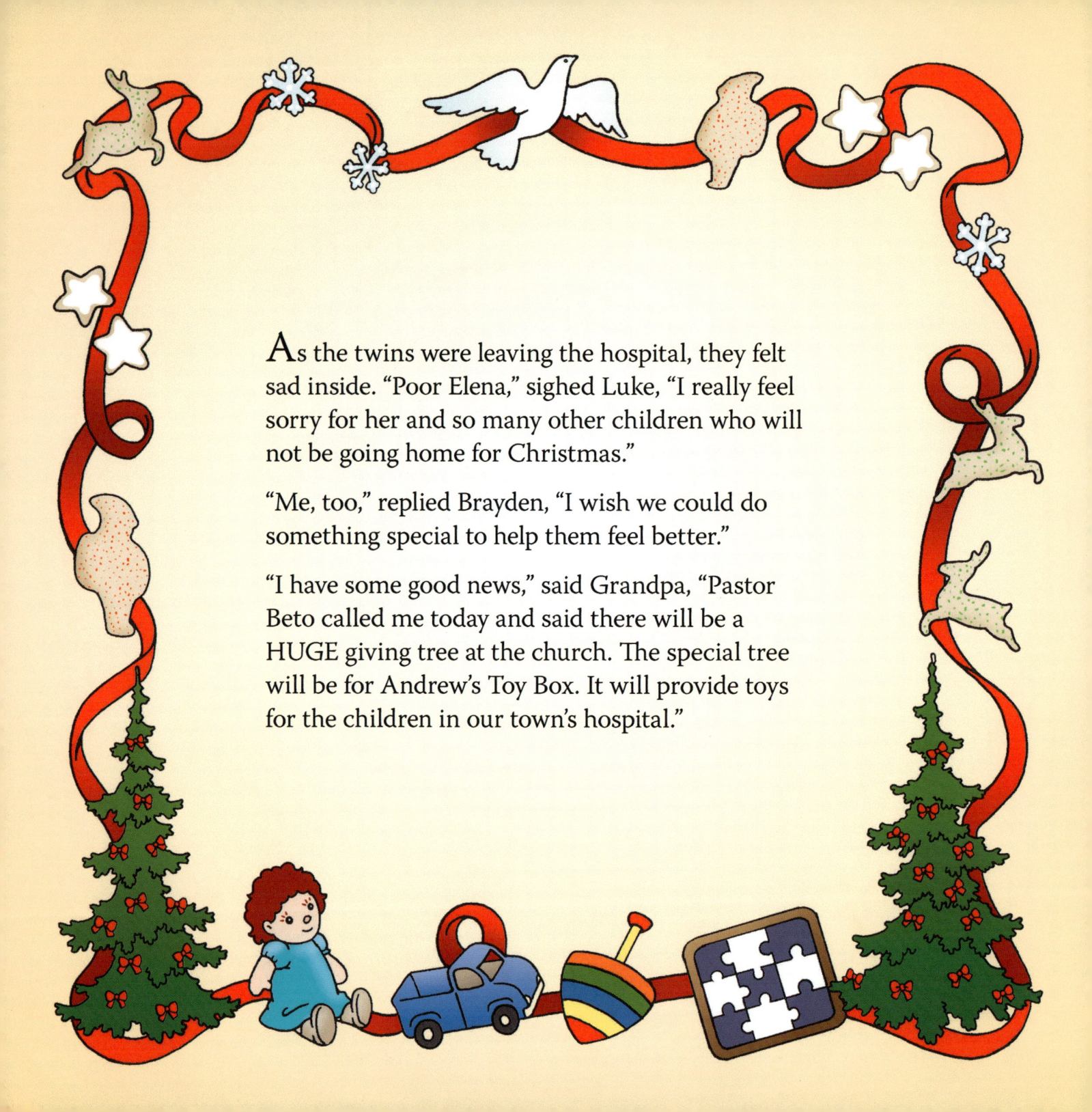

As the twins were leaving the hospital, they felt sad inside. "Poor Elena," sighed Luke, "I really feel sorry for her and so many other children who will not be going home for Christmas."

"Me, too," replied Brayden, "I wish we could do something special to help them feel better."

"I have some good news," said Grandpa, "Pastor Beto called me today and said there will be a HUGE giving tree at the church. The special tree will be for Andrew's Toy Box. It will provide toys for the children in our town's hospital."

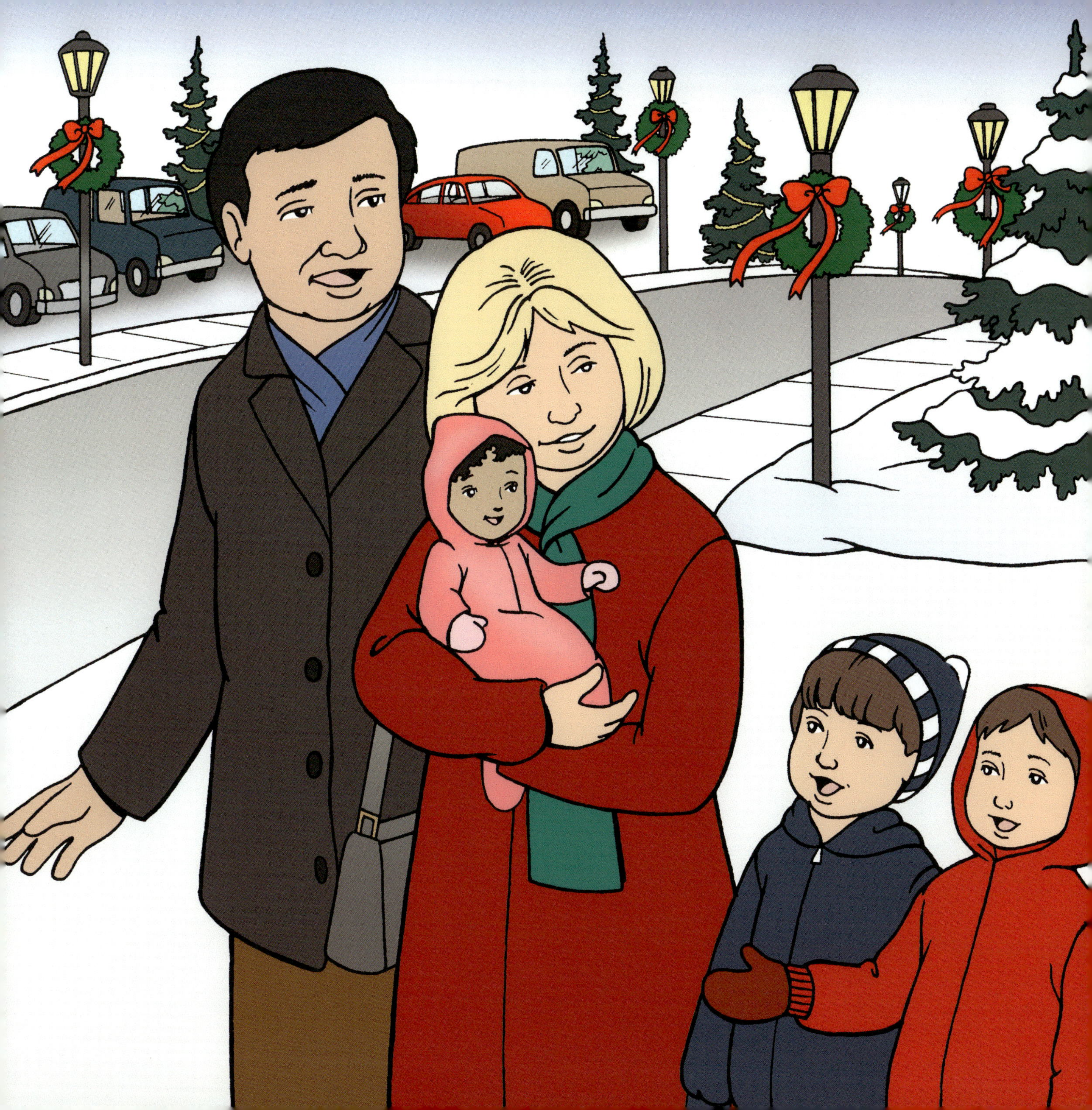

"What is a special giving tree, Grandpa?" asked Luke.

"A giving tree is a holiday tree decorated with pretty tags instead of ornaments," answered Grandpa.

"Why are there tags?" asked Brayden.

"They are labeled with names of toys for children in need. Everyone picks a colorful tag, buys the special toy, and puts it under the tree. Then, the gifts will be delivered to the hospital," explained Grandpa.

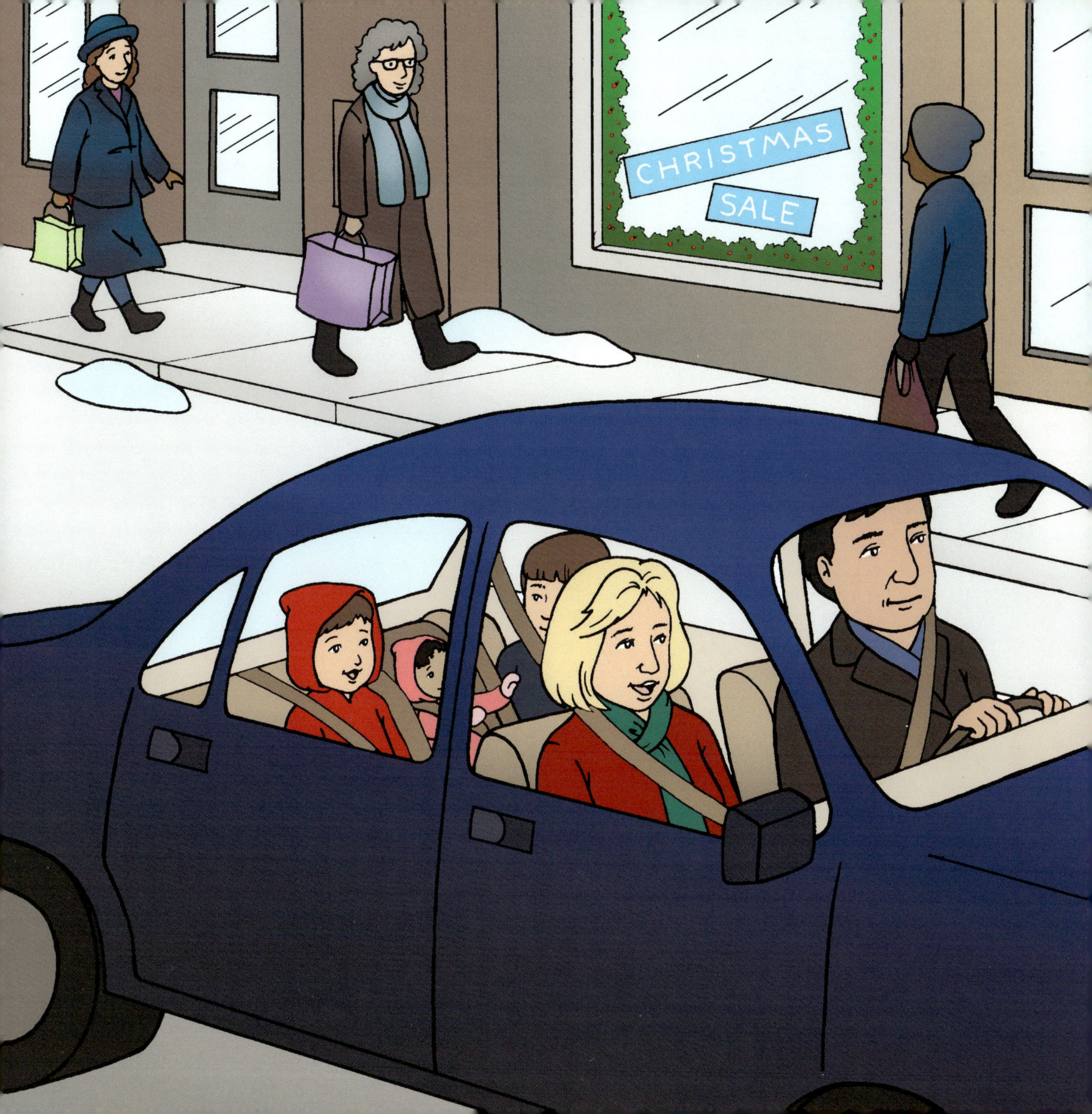
CHRISTMAS
SALE

"Can we make some tags for the children we saw today?" Luke wanted to know.

"Yes, we will go to church tomorrow to help the Youth Group fill the tree with tags," answered Grandma.

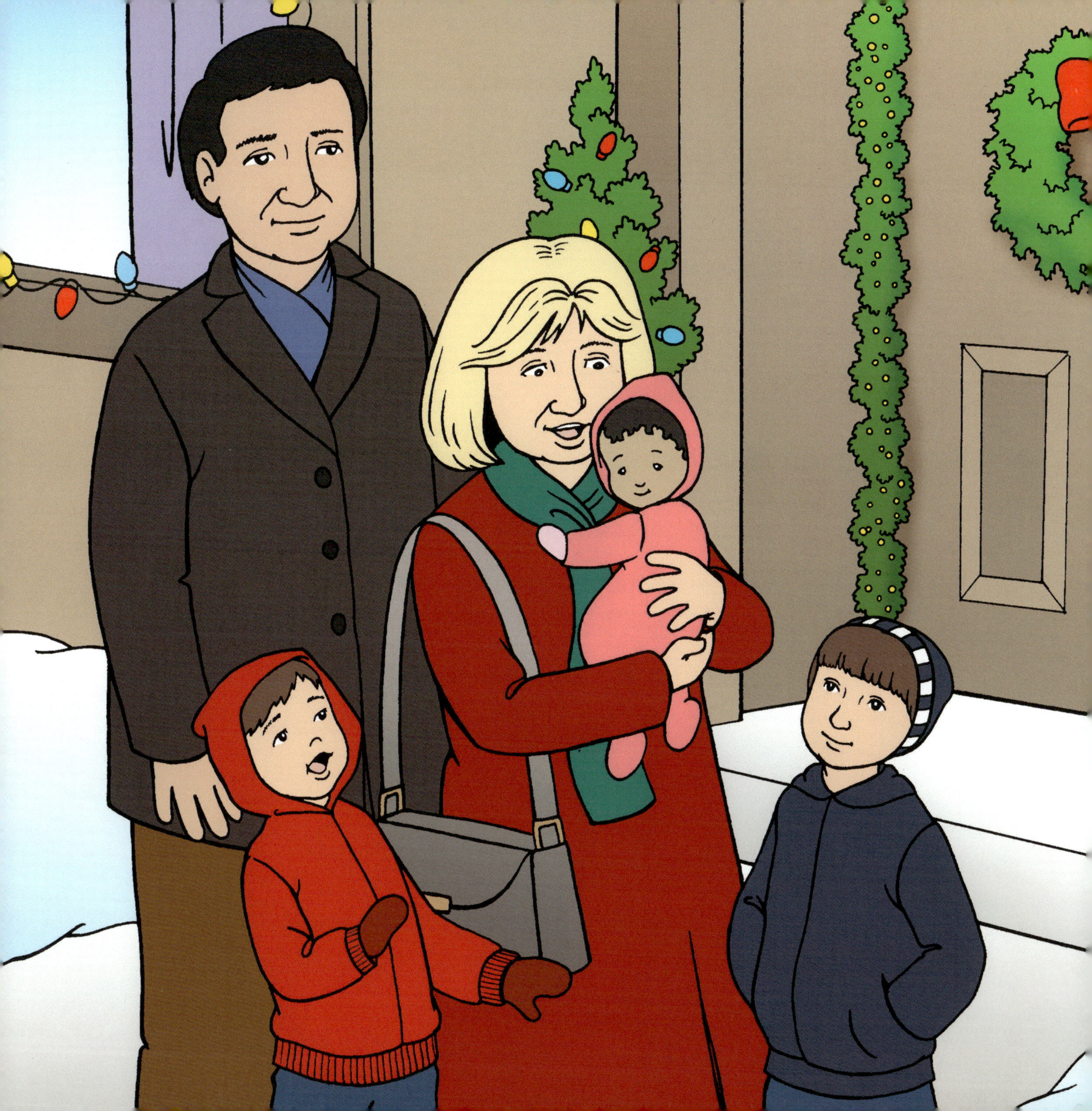

Brayden and Luke could hardly wait to arrive at church the next morning. They were thrilled to see their cousins, Richie, Christy, and Caleb, who were already busy decorating the tree with the Youth Group. The twins happily helped hang the brightly colored tags and noticed the smiling faces of everyone as they finished the dazzling giving tree.

At that moment, Pastor Beto came in to see the beautiful tree and said, "Ooh, it looks fantastic! Do you all know the amazing giving tree secret?" Everyone looked at each other, but no one had a clue what the secret could be. "Just watch and see what happens," he said with a twinkle in his eye.

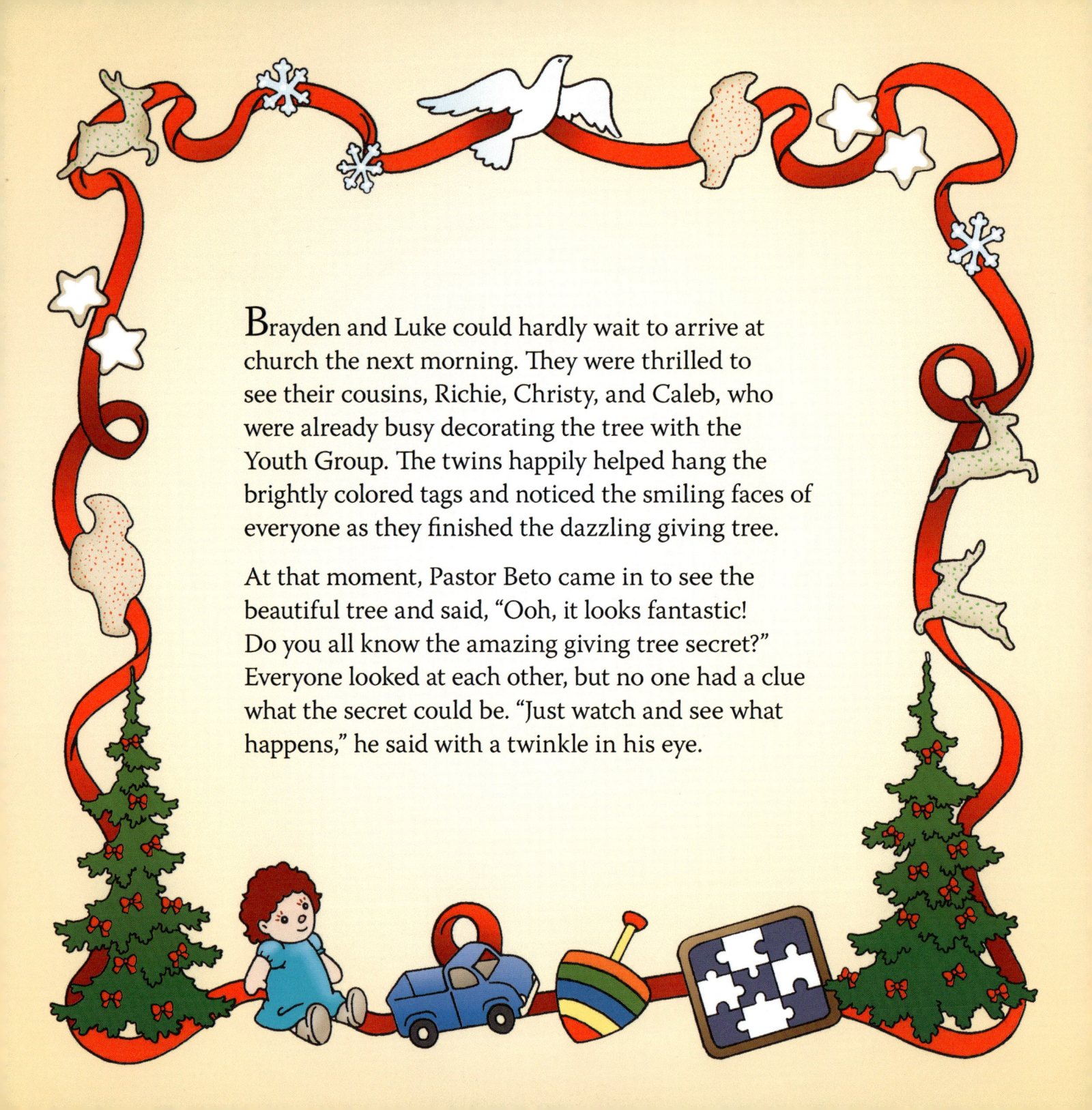

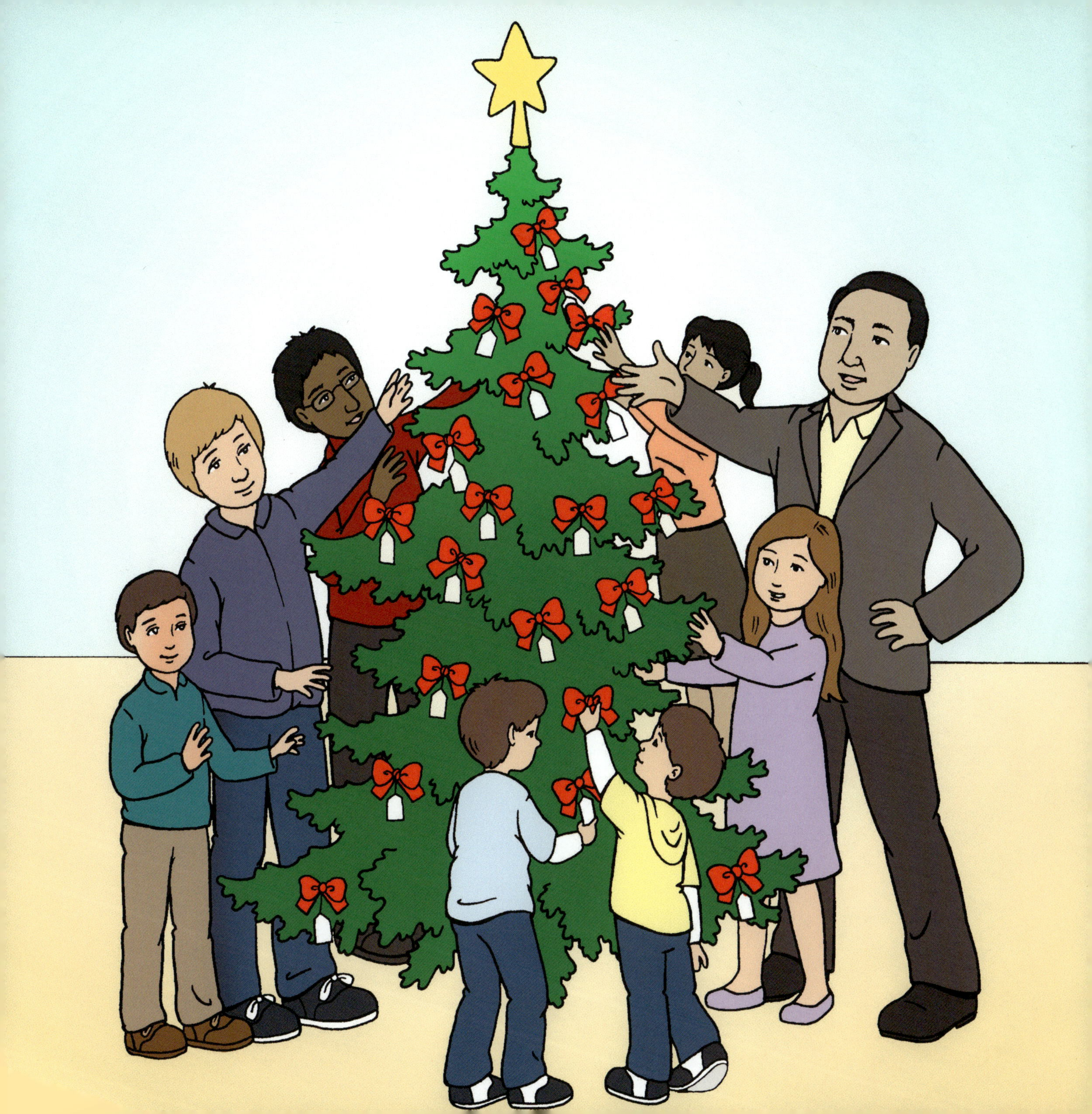

Later that morning, the people eagerly began taking the tags from the tree. "Our church friends look more excited than ever," said Luke.

"They surely do," replied Brayden, grinning from ear to ear.

The curious twins kept trying to discover the secret of the giving tree but they just couldn't solve the mystery.

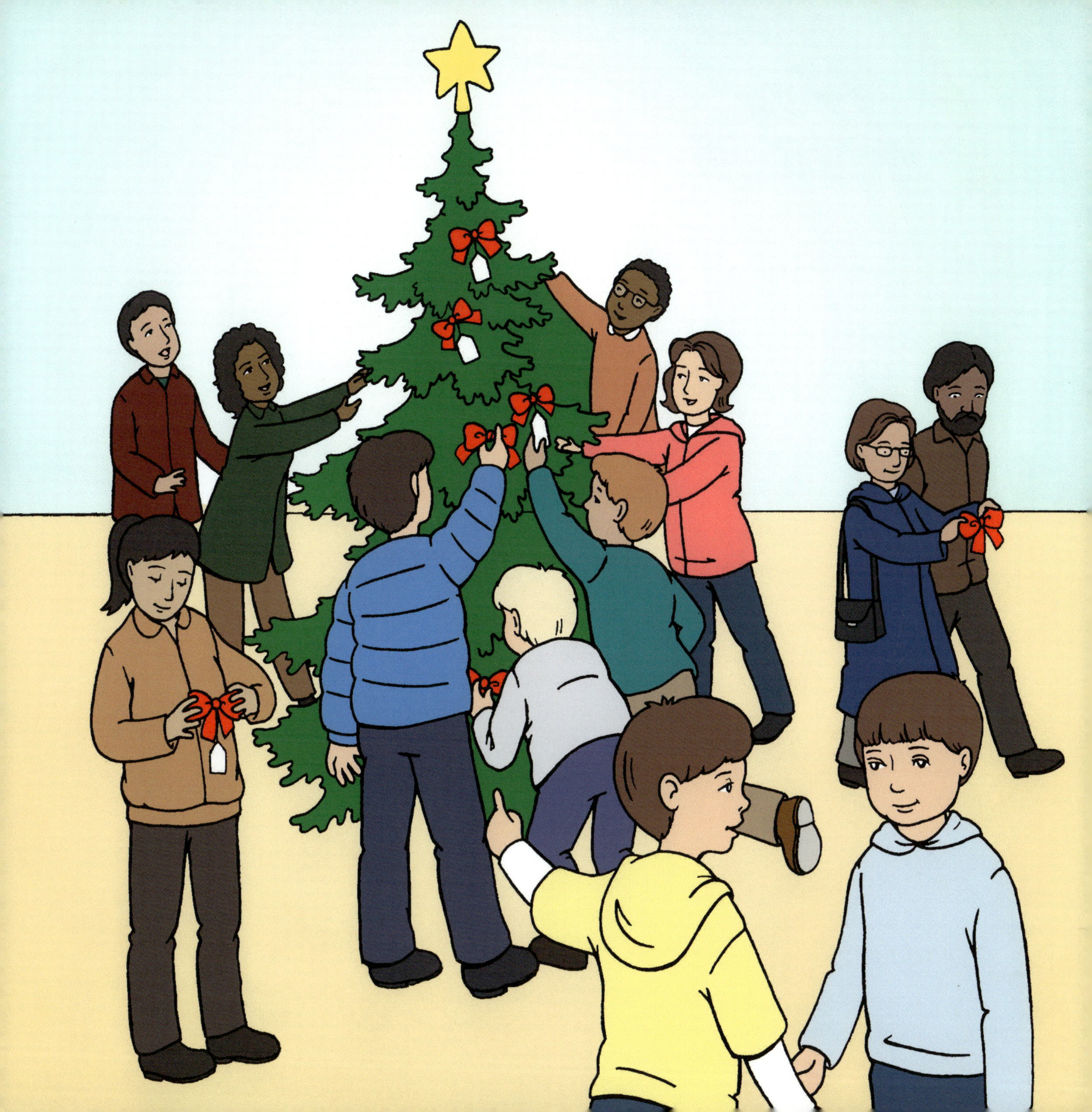

The next Sunday, Luke and Brayden hurried into the church and saw the overwhelming joy and love of each person bringing a special present to the tree. The bottom of the giving tree overflowed with wonderful surprises.

"Oh boy, this is awesome," shouted Brayden, "there are plenty of toys for all the sick children!"

Christmas Eve had finally come. It was now time to deliver the many gifts to the hospital.

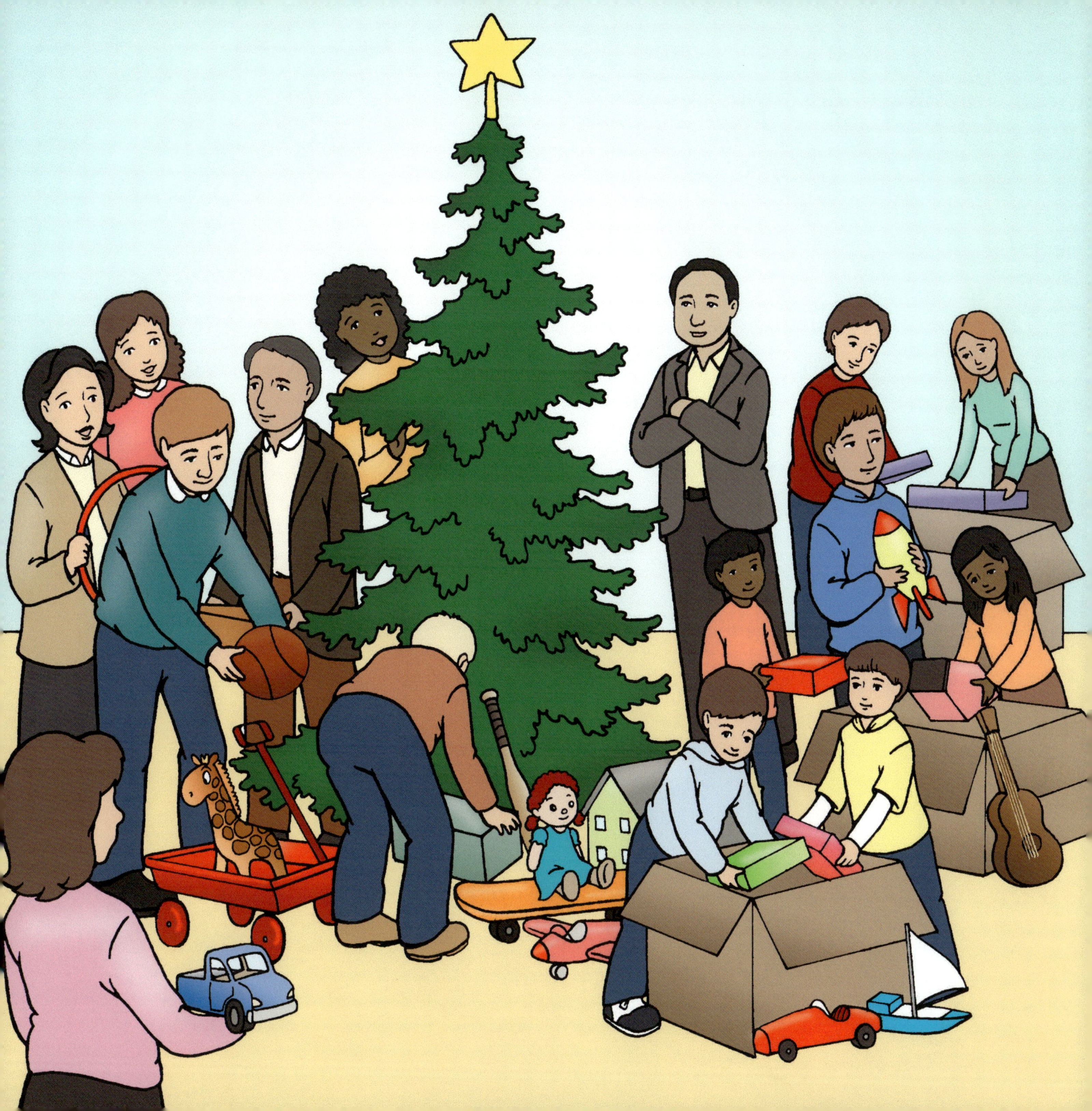

The twins, their cousins, and the youth group felt as merry as Santa's elves when they arrived at the hospital. The sick children's eyes sparkled like Christmas stars when they received their toys. Elena hugged the cuddly kitty that purred, "Meow, Meow." "He looks exactly like my real kitten at home," she said in disbelief. "Your kind visit and special gifts have made my Christmas wonderful, after all," she lovingly said. Elena's face beamed with happiness.

After the toys had been delivered, Luke exclaimed, "I think I've discovered the amazing giving tree secret! Is it kindness, love and joy?"

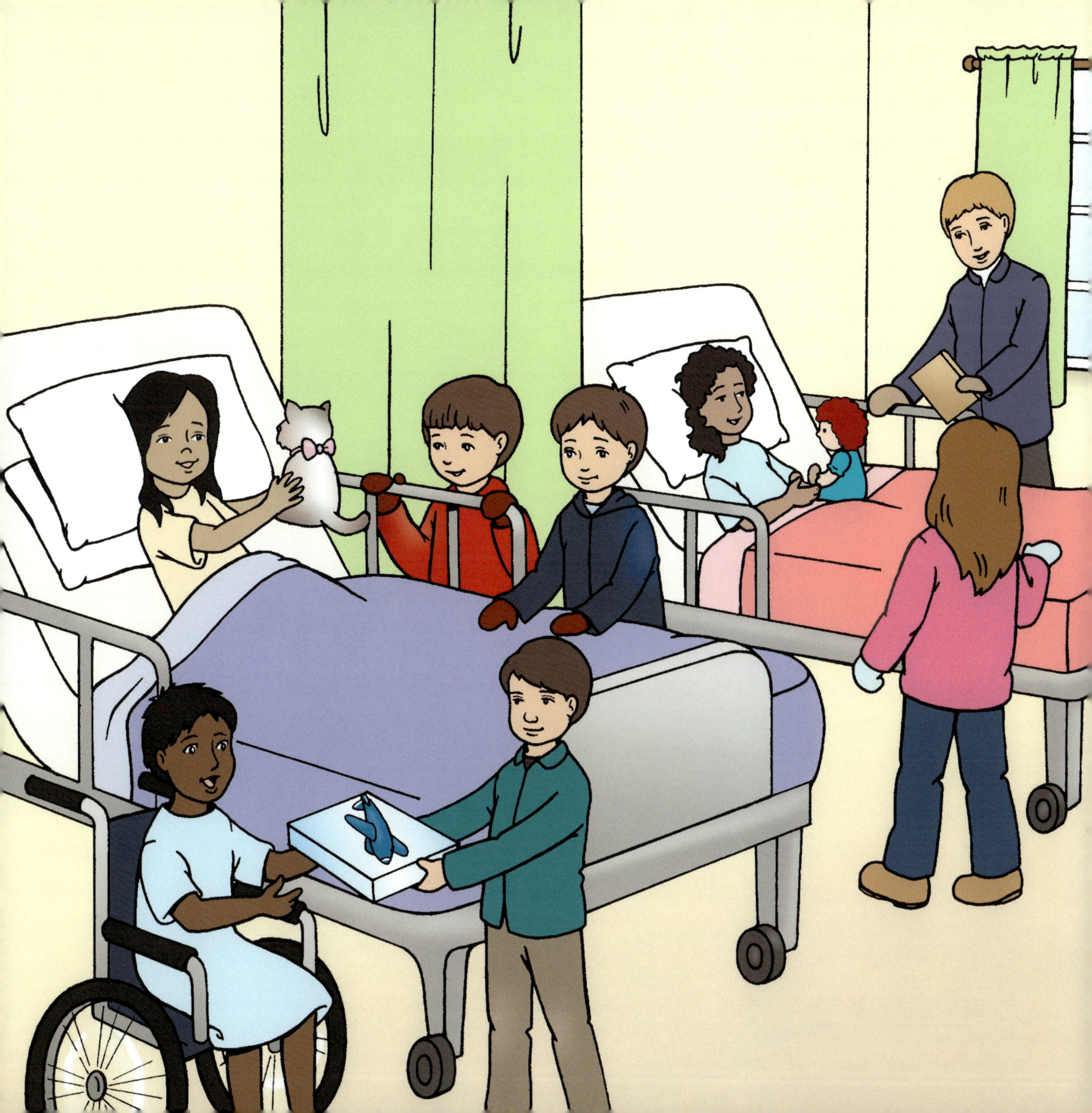

Grandma smiled and replied, "Sure enough, that's it exactly! You were all so kind to make the tags and decorate the giving tree. The church members were filled with love when they took the tags and brought the gifts. We felt special joy when we delivered the toys to the hospital. The sick children were thrilled to receive their surprises."

"WOW, Grandma, the giving tree gave everyone something! What an Amazing Tree!" Brayden said, jumping up and down.

"I love this warm feeling in my heart, Grandpa," said Luke.

"That is the feeling of caring, giving, and loving," Grandpa replied. "You see, when you give to others and help those in need, you become a reflection of Jesus' love. His goodness shines through you."

What fun it was to bring the gift of joy to Elena and so many sick children in the town's hospital! Everyone had, indeed, discovered THE AMAZING GIVING TREE SECRET.

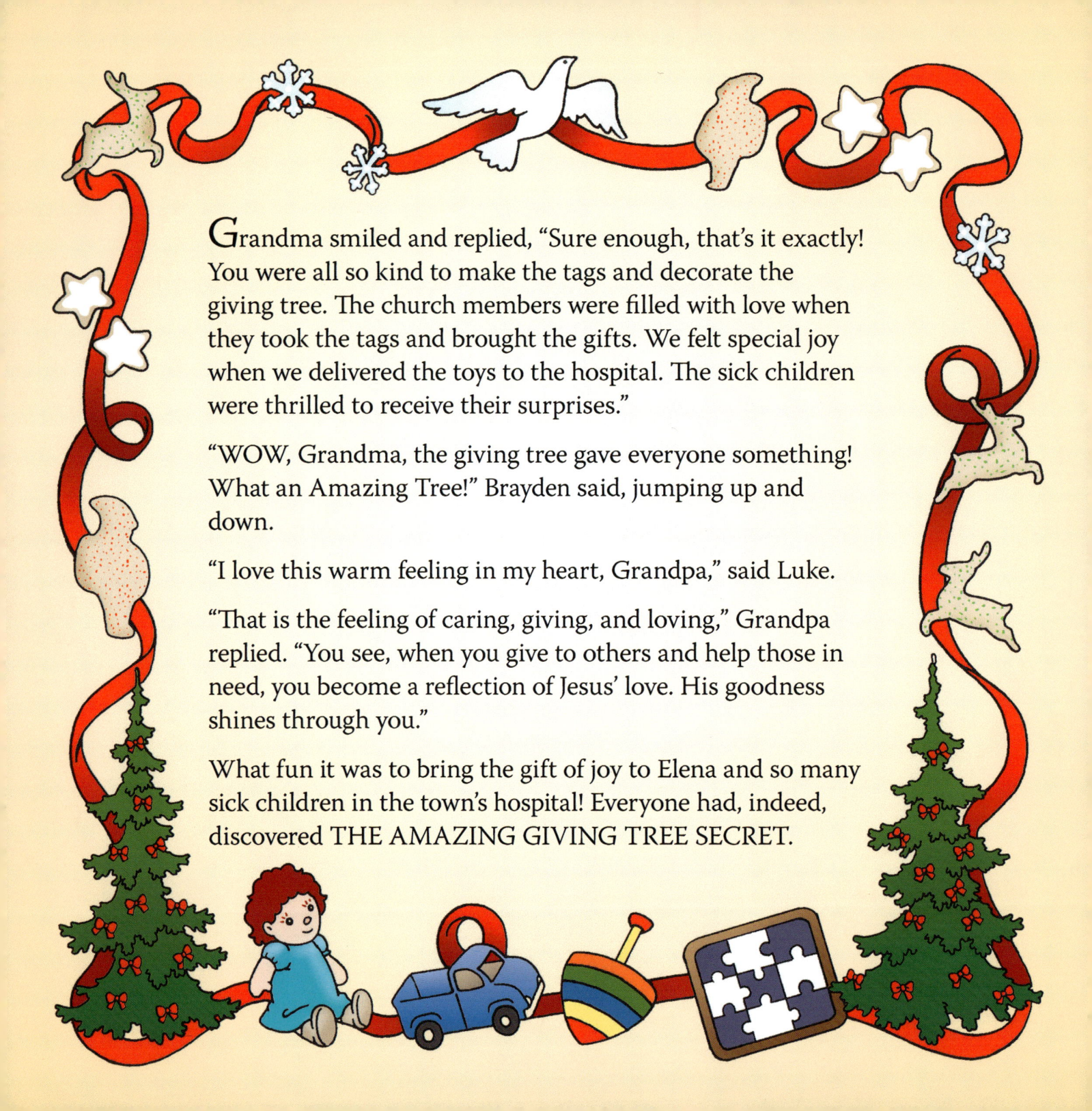

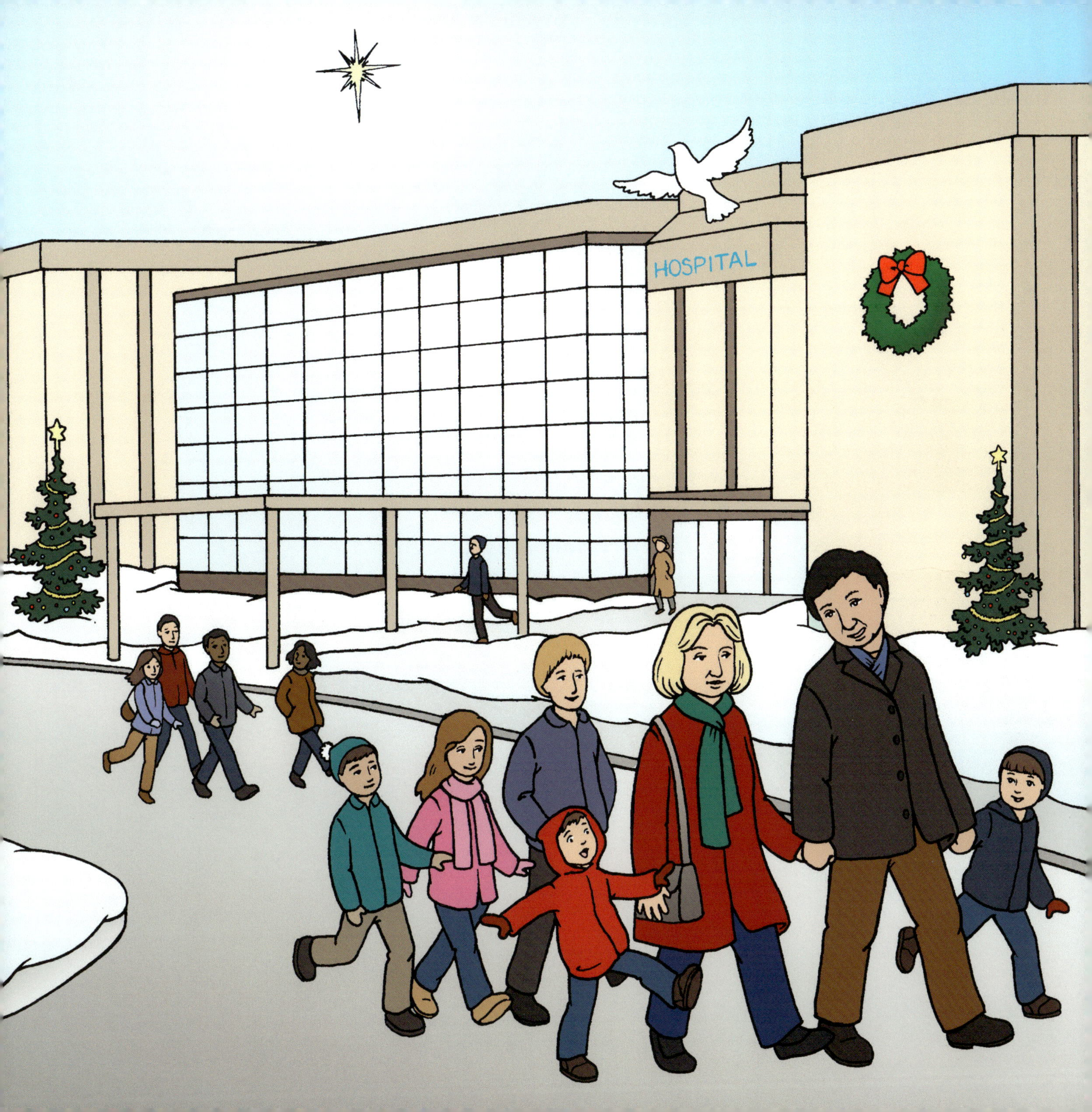
HOSPITAL

Experience the amazing giving tree secret. Make a difference in your life and the lives of others by creating a giving tree in your community. The giving tree concept may be used during any season and for any holiday to benefit your special cause. Visit www.andrewstoybox.org and click on The Giving Tree for more information.

Acknowledgements

Tremendous appreciation to my husband, Richard; sons, Rich and John and their families; my sister, Michelle, and my mentor, Barbara Rodgers for their amazing support and assistance in making this book a reality.

CPSIA information can be obtained
at www.ICGtesting.com
Printed in the USA
LVIC05n1407241113
362488LV00002B/2

9 781462 706440